Baby's
First Year

A keepsake journal of milestone moments

annabel karmel

DK

introduction

"With this first year album you will be able to record all the precious moments you spend with your baby in the first 12 months, from the quirky little things that your baby does to the first smile and the very first wobbly steps. Along with your prenatal scans, lock of your baby's hair, and favorite photos, this book will keep those memories alive forever—not only as a keepsake for you, but something that your child will treasure in the years to come." *Annabel*

LONDON, NEW YORK, MELBOURNE, MUNICH, AND DELHI

Project editor Helen Murray

Project art editors Sara Kimmins and Peggy Sadler

Designer Jo Grey

Production editor Jenny Woodcock

Production controller Alice Holloway

Managing editors Penny Warren and Esther Ripley

Managing art editor Marianne Markham

Illustrator Simon Abbott

Creative technical support Sonia Charbonnier

Category publisher Peggy Vance

First American edition, 2008

Published in the United States by
DK Publishing
345 Hudson Street
New York, New York 10014

16 11

020-BD617-Apr/08

Copyright © 2008 Dorling Kindersley Limited
Text copyright © 2008 Annabel Karmel
All rights reserved

Without limiting the rights under copyright reserved above, no part of this publication may be reproduced, stored in or introduced into a retrieval system, or transmitted, in any form, or by any means (electronic, mechanical, photocopying, recording, or otherwise), without the prior written permission of both the copyright owner and the above publisher of this book.

Published in Great Britain by Dorling Kindersley Limited.

A catalog record for this book is available from the Library of Congress.

ISBN 978-0-7566-3723-1

DK books are available at special discounts when purchased in bulk for sales promotions, premiums, fund-raising, or educational use. For details, contact: DK Publishing Special Markets, 345 Hudson Street, New York, New York 10014 or SpecialSales@dk.com.

Printed and bound in China

Discover more at
www.dk.com

this book is all about

....

my parents

" One day you're just a couple and the next you're a family. Within the space of 12 months, you won't be able to imagine life without your baby. Nurture your baby, enjoy seeing a reflection of yourselves in her, and ultimately encourage her to grow to be herself. **"** *Annabel*

how mommy met daddy ....
....
....

mommy's food cravings during pregnancy ....
....
....

what mommy was doing when she went into labor ....
....
....
....

what daddy was doing when mommy went into labor ....
....
....
....

mommy's name ....   daddy's name ....
....

mommy's birth date ....   daddy's birth date ....

mommy's place of birth ....   daddy's place of birth ....
....

mommy's astrological sign ....   daddy's astrological sign ....

mommy's eye color ....   daddy's eye color ....

mommy's hair color ....   daddy's hair color ....

mommy's job ....   daddy's job ....
....

mommy's hobbies ....   daddy's hobbies ....
....

my family tree

"Whether traditional or exotic, your baby's name is a unique gift that many believe will shape his personality. In years to come he will enjoy looking at his family tree and reading all about his name." *Annabel*

the name I was given ....

....

what my name means ....

....

....

the reason why my name was chosen ....

....

....

the names I might have been given ....

....

....

famous people who share my name ....

....

great
grandparents

....

....

great
grandparents

....

....

great
grandparents

....

....

great
grandparents

....

....

grandfather

....

grandmother

....

grandfather

....

grandmother

....

aunts/uncles

....

....

....

mother

father

aunts/uncles

....

....

....

brothers

....

....

me

....

sisters

....

....

other family members

....

....

....

sharing the news

" The best part of a newly discovered pregnancy is sharing it with others. Some people wait until after the first 12 weeks, while others share the news immediately. As you get closer to your delivery date, there will be opportunities to celebrate—a leaving party at work, a celebration with family and friends, or a baby shower your friends may have organized for you. " *Annabel*

how the news was celebrated ....
....
....

who my parents celebrated with ....
....
....

presents received ....
....
....

a birth announcement card
or celebration card

my birth

" It's a magical moment when you first set eyes on your baby. It's the start of a journey for all of you. This precious time is all too brief though, so don't wish it away. Treasure the special moments of life with your newborn baby. " *Annabel*

I was born on ....

at this time ....

at this place ....

the labor lasted ....

I weighed ....

I measured ....

my eyes were ....

my hair was ....

people at the birth ....
....

my first visitors ....
....

mommy's and daddy's thoughts when they first saw me ....
....
....
....
....

an envelope for a lock of hair and
other keepsakes

my first few days

66 It's good to keep your baby close and involve her in your daily life, so set aside a small, cozy space for your baby wherever you are. She'll spend much of her time asleep and she'll be able to sleep just about anywhere. A bassinet or carry crib is best at first, and easily portable. 99 *Annabel*

I came home on ....

my first address ....
....

my visitors ....
....
....

gifts I received ....
....

....

....

....

my feeding patterns in my first week ....

....

....

how I slept in my first week ....

....

how my parents felt in the first week ......

....

....

....

....

about my world

" Use these pages to record a snapshot of the world your baby was born into. In years to come, you'll enjoy looking back and sharing these times with your child, and you'll no doubt laugh together at some of the things you've written below. " *Annabel*

news headlines ....
....
....
....
....
....

president or prime minister ....

movies ....
....
....

movie stars ....
....
....
....
....

television shows ....

....

hit songs ....

....

pop stars and groups ....

....

big names in sports ....

....

bestselling books ....

fashion trends ....

....

the price of things:
milk ....

gallon of gas ....

postage stamp ....

a photo of me
in the bath

date taken ....

bathtime

"You may think bathtime is about washing, but in truth it's more about splashing, kicking, and having fun. Treasure this special time, when you can wrap your baby in a hooded towel and cuddle him dry." *Annabel*

about my first bath ....
....
....
....

the first time I went in the big bath ....
....
....
....

my favorite bathtime toys ....
....
....

my favorite bathtub games ....
....
....
....

bedtime

> Do you remember uninterrupted nights of blissful sleep? Whoever coined the phrase "sleeping like a baby" obviously didn't have one. Here's a chance to record some of your baby's nocturnal antics. **Annabel**

about my bassinet ....

I first moved to a big crib ....

I first slept through the night ....

my evening routine in my first year ....
....

my favorite bedtime toys ....
....

my bedtime books ....
....
....

my lullabies ....
....

a photo of me
at bedtime

date taken ....

my first teeth

" The first tooth can appear at any time in the first year. While some babies sail through teething, it can be more difficult for others. When each tooth comes through, write the number on the diagram and then write the date next to the number. **"** *Annabel*

date   date

upper

right   left

lower

what I was like during teething ....

....

my favorite teething toy ....

my hair

" Some babies are born with a full head of hair, while others are completely bald. Their hair may also rub off to reveal an entirely different color underneath. Every baby is different, but many have their first haircut at about a year old. " *Annabel*

my hair at birth ....

my hair at 6 months ....

my hair at 1 year ....

I most closely resemble ....

date of my first haircut ....

who cut it? ....

how much was cut? ....
....

what I thought about it ....
....
....

on the move

" The physical skills your baby develops in the first year are remarkable and she will be a constant delight as she reaches these important milestones. Use this page to record the excitement of your baby's firsts. **"** *Annabel*

I lifted my head ....

I started to roll over ....

I found my feet ....

I managed to sit up alone ....

I began to crawl or bottom-shuffle ....
....

I learned to clap ....

I pulled myself up to standing ....
....

I took my first steps ....
....

a photo of me
on the move

date taken ....

a photo of me smiling, singing, or babbling

date taken ....

talking

" Babies need and want to communicate from their earliest days. Even before they can vocalize, they listen to and try to imitate sounds. It's lovely to have a record of your baby's first words and expressions. It's amazing how quickly you forget them. " *Annabel*

the first time I smiled ....

my first noises ....
....

things that made me laugh ....
....

my best babbling noises ....
....

I first tried to sing ....

my first word was ....

when I said it ....

at 12 months I could say ....
....
....

family and friends

" You and your baby share a special bond. Through you he'll come to understand the pleasure of social interaction and communication. He'll soon learn to recognize family and friends and will delight in meeting and being with other people. " *Annabel*

special things I do with mommy ....

....

special things I do with daddy ....

....

what I like to do with other people in my family ....

....

....

my baby friends ....

I first kissed mommy and daddy ....

I learned to wave ....

I first played peek-a-boo ....

a photo of me with special people

date taken ....

first tastes

"Babies grow more rapidly in their first year than at any other time in their life. Don't go for baby food in jars with a shelf life of two years. Fresh food is best and it's as easy as mashing a banana or steaming some carrots." *Annabel*

I first tried solids ....

what I thought of them ....
....

my favorite fruit purées ....
....

my favorite vegetable purées ....
....

unusual things I tried ....

foods I disliked ....
....

foods I'm allergic to ....
....

apple and pear with cinnamon

Apple and pear purée is an ideal first food because it's easy to digest and unlikely to cause allergies. Choose sweet apples like Baldwin, Rome Beauty, or Cortland. Apples and pears contain pectin, which can slow things down if your baby has loose bowel motions.

2 apples, peeled, cored, and sliced

2 ripe pears (e.g. Bartlett), peeled, cored, and sliced

4 tbsp pure unsweetened apple juice or water

a pinch of ground cinnamon (optional)

1 Put the fruit into a saucepan together with the apple juice or water. Bring to a boil, reduce the heat, cover, and simmer gently until tender (about 6 minutes).

2 Purée in a blender or food processor.

makes 4 portions

suitable for freezing

preparation time: 5 minutes

cooking time: 6 minutes

trio of root vegetables

Root vegetables are a great choice for a first food because they have a naturally sweet taste, can be puréed to a smooth consistency, and are unlikely to cause allergies. Sweet potato, in particular, is a good source of vitamin C and betacarotene and is richer in nutrients than ordinary potatoes. Rutabaga and pumpkin are tasty too.

1 small sweet potato, about 8oz (225g), peeled and cut into small chunks

2 medium-sized carrots, about 8oz (225g), peeled and sliced

1 small parsnip, about 4oz (115g), peeled and chopped

1 Put the vegetables in a steamer over a pan of simmering water (to retain maximum nutrients) or in a saucepan with just enough boiling water to cover, and cook for 15 minutes until tender. Drain, if necessary, reserving the water.

2 Purée the vegetables in a blender, adding about 5 tbsp of the boiled water from the bottom of the steamer or saucepan, or some of your baby's usual milk, to make a soft consistency for your baby.

makes 6 portions

suitable for freezing

preparation time: 8 minutes

cooking time: 15 minutes

first meals

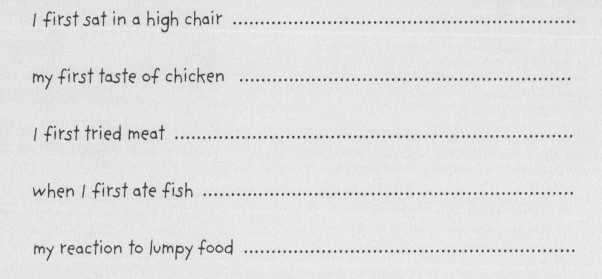

66 From the age of six months, babies need more than just fruit and vegetables. They need meat or lentils for iron, and fish for essential fatty acids. Introduce your baby to lumpy foods from an early age—older babies will find it harder to accept lumps. 99 *Annabel*

I first sat in a high chair ....

my first taste of chicken ....

I first tried meat ....

when I first ate fish ....

my reaction to lumpy food ....

I first drank from a cup ....
....

I like to drink ....
....

I first held a spoon ....
....

tasty salmon with sweet potato

Oily fish contains essential fatty acids, which are important for a baby's developing brain and eyesight. In the first year, a baby's brain triples in size and a large part of the brain is made up of fatty acids. It is true that eating fish can make us smarter and including omega-3s in a child's diet not only improves their ability to concentrate and learn, but can also help children with dyspraxia, dyslexia, and ADHD.

1 fairly large sweet potato, about 10oz (300g), peeled and cut into small chunks

4½oz (125g) salmon fillet, skinned

2 tbsp milk

1 tbsp butter

¾ cup roughly chopped tomatoes, skin and seeds removed

⅓ cup Cheddar cheese, grated

1 Put the sweet potato into a steamer over a pan of simmering water, cover, and cook for about 10 minutes.

2 Meanwhile, make sure there are no bones left in the salmon and place it in a microwavable dish. Add the milk and dot with a quarter of the butter. Cover, leaving an air vent, and microwave on high for about 2 minutes, or until the fish is just cooked and flakes easily. Alternatively, put the salmon in a small pan, add enough milk to just cover the fish and a quarter of the butter, and simmer for about 4 minutes or until cooked.

3 Melt the remaining butter in a saucepan, stir in the chopped tomatoes, and sauté for about 2 minutes, stirring, until softened. Remove from the heat and stir in the cheese until melted.

4 Put the fish, plus the cooking liquid, into a blender together with the sweet potato and cheese and tomato mixture. Blend until smooth. If it is too thick, add a little more milk. For older babies, mash the sweet potato with the tomato and cheese sauce, and flake in the salmon.

TIP An easy way to skin tomatoes is to slit the skin, cover with boiling water for 1 minute, strain, and rinse under cold water. The skins should peel off easily.

makes 4 portions

suitable for freezing

preparation time: 10 minutes

cooking time: 10 minutes

feeding myself

❝ Toward the end of the first year babies often go through a difficult stage where they refuse to be spoonfed and reject anything with lumps in it. However, they will happily chew on finger foods, like carrot or cucumber sticks. Odd, isn't it? ❞ Annabel

my favorite finger foods ....
....

the things I do with my food ....
....
....

my favorite home-made recipes ....
....
....

what I eat for breakfast ....
....
....

my special treats ....
....

poached chicken balls

It's good to make finger foods that contain protein. Traditionally cooked meatballs can be a little too chewy for first finger foods, but poaching them in stock makes them soft and tender—perfect for little ones. The idea for these came from Italian "Wedding Soup," where meatballs are poached and served in soup. Serve with steamed baby carrots and broccoli florets, or for older children, with tomato sauce.

1 shallot, diced (about 1½ tbsp)

1 tsp olive oil

1 slice of bread, crusts removed

4oz (115g) ground chicken

¼ sweet eating apple, peeled, cored, and coarsely grated

3 tbsp grated Parmesan cheese

¼ tsp chopped fresh thyme leaves

pepper (optional)

2 cups low-salt chicken stock

1 Sauté the shallot in the oil for 3–4 minutes until soft. Transfer to the bowl of a food processor and leave to cool for a few minutes.

2 Tear the bread and, with the food processor running, add the bread to the onions, a piece at a time, to make breadcrumbs.

3 Add the chicken, apple, Parmesan, and thyme and season with a little pepper if you wish. Whiz until well combined. Roll teaspoonfuls of the mixture into balls and set aside. (It will be less sticky if you dampen your hands with cold water.)

4 Put the stock into a medium-sized saucepan and bring to a boil. Add the chicken balls and bring back to a boil. Reduce the heat and poach gently for 4 minutes, until cooked through. Remove with a slotted spoon and cool for several minutes before serving. Cut the balls in half for smaller babies.

5 To reheat a single portion (3–7 balls), put the balls in a small bowl and add a teaspoon of water. Cover and cook in a microwave on high for 20–40 seconds, until piping hot. Do not overcook or they will turn rubbery. Allow to cool before serving.

makes about 21 balls (3–7 servings, depending on age and appetite)

suitable for freezing

preparation time: 15 minutes

cooking time: 10 minutes

outings and vacations

" Your first outing with your baby is likely to be a major event, but you'll be folding the stroller into the car or getting off the bus with bags full of groceries in no time. Treasure seeing your baby's excited face as your outings and trips away become more adventurous. " *Annabel*

about my first outing ....

....

....

my first trip to the park or playground ....

....

my favorite activity ....

my first outing on a train ....

my first outing on a bus ....

....

my first swim ....

....

my first party ....

....

my party outfit ....

my first vacation or trip ....

....

I went with ....

what I loved ....

....

what I hated ....

....

....

special occasions

" Use this page to record the events of a special day, such as a Christening or naming day or your baby's first Christmas, Diwali, Hanukkah, or other religious holiday. Even though your baby won't remember this day, she'll enjoy reading all about it and looking at the photos in years to come. " *Annabel*

my special day ....

....

the place ....

the guests ....

....

I wore ....

presents I received ....

....

....

memories from the day ....

....

a photo of me on
a special day

date taken ....

1 month

"By one month your baby is gaining more control of her body and losing some of the jerky movements of a newborn baby. She loves to gaze at your face and recognizes the sound of your voice and will know your smell. She will enjoy gazing at a mobile above her crib." *Annabel*

things I can do ....
....

funny noises I make ....
....

I cry when ....
....

how my parents keep me quiet ....
....

funny things I do ....
....

how I've been sleeping ....
....

a photo of me
at 1 month

weight ....
length ....

2 months

"Your baby is spending more time awake and is learning that he can make things happen—he may try to swipe at a toy. You'll notice he gets excited in anticipation of bathtime and feeding. He likes to suck on almost anything and enjoys looking at himself in a mirror." *Annabel*

new things I can do ....

....

funny noises I make ....

....

I smile when ....

....

....

cute things I do ....

....

my feeding patterns ....

....

my favorite lullabies ....

....

a photo of me
at 2 months

weight ....
length ....

3 months

"Your baby may grasp a rattle and shake it, but she can't pick it up by herself yet. She can see objects at a distance more clearly now and will follow you with her eyes as you move around the room. She can also imitate exaggerated facial expressions. Playmats with different textures and sounds are a great way to entertain your baby." *Annabel*

new things I can do ....

....

toys I enjoy playing with ....

....

games I like to play ....

....

funny things I do ....

....

my favorite way to be held ....

....

how I've been sleeping ....

....

a photo of me
at 3 months

weight ....
length ....

4 months

"Your baby will try to grab objects within reach and start to bring everything toward his mouth. He is beginning to realize that he can make things happen, so enjoys toys that respond to his actions with loud noises or bright lights. He likes books with large, colorful, simple pictures." *Annabel*

new things I can do ....
....

I smile when ....
....

baby groups I go to ....
....

my favorite bedtime toys ....
....

places I've been to ....
....

cute things I do ....
....

a photo of me
at 4 months

weight ....
length ....

5 months

> "When held in a standing position your baby may be able to support her weight on her legs and will enjoy bouncing up and down. Her body language is becoming more expressive. She'll put everything in her mouth, so avoid toys with small parts—soft balls are a good choice at this age." *Annabel*

new things I can do ....

....

my favorite toys ....

....

games I like to play ....

....

I laugh when ....

....

funny things I do ....

....

my favorite things to cuddle ....

....

a photo of me
at 5 months

weight ....
length ....

6 months

"Your baby may now be able to sit without support and can reach for and grab objects. He may start to recognize names and simple words. He will babble and imitate some of your sounds and will enjoy playing "peek-a-boo." At around six months he'll be introduced to his first solid foods." *Annabel*

new things I can do ....

....

favorite bathtime toys ....

how I've been sleeping ....

....

my friends ....

....

foods I like ....

foods I dislike ....

....

a photo of me
at 6 months

weight ....
length ....

7 months

" Your baby will be getting to grips with finger foods and will enjoy lifting her foot to her mouth to suck her toes too. She is able to sense if you are happy or annoyed by the tone of your voice and will begin to understand the meaning of "no." She will chuckle at pop-up toys and other surprises. "

Annabel

new things I can do ....

....

my favorite toys ....

....

games I like to play ....

....

places I've been to ....

....

I laugh when ....

....

cute things I do ....

....

....

a photo of me
at 7 months

weight ....
length ....

8 months

"As soon as your baby can pick up objects with his thumb and forefinger, feeding himself becomes much more fun. He should be able to stand while holding on to something and point to things that he wants. His babble may sound like "mama" and "dada," but you'll have to wait a little longer to hear his first real words." *Annabel*

new things I can do ....
....

my favorite book ....
....

my friends ....
....

funny things I do ....
....

foods I like ....
....

foods I dislike ....
....

a photo of me
at 8 months

weight ....
length ....

9 months

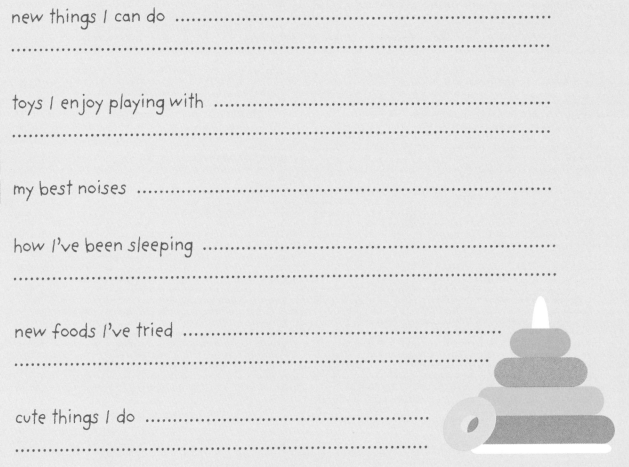

"Your baby may be able to crawl or bottom-shuffle and even pull herself up to standing to start to cruise around the room, holding on to furniture. She will now have more coordinated hand movements and may be able to build a tower of two blocks and put stacking rings on a spindle." *Annabel*

new things I can do ....
....

toys I enjoy playing with ....
....

my best noises ....

how I've been sleeping ....
....

new foods I've tried ....
....

cute things I do ....
....

a photo of me
at 9 months

weight ....
length ....

10 months

"By around 10 months your baby will be eager to feed himself and may prefer finger foods. He can understand far more than he can say and will recognize words like "shoe" and "drink." As his concentration improves, he will be able to play with more challenging toys." *Annabel*

new things I can do ....
....

words I understand ....
....

my friends ....
....

my favorite activity ....
....

foods I like ....
....

things I dislike ....
....

a photo of me
at 10 months

weight ....
length ....

11 months

"Your baby may be fully mobile, moving from place to place by crawling or cruising around the furniture. Sit-and-ride toys are a great choice at this age and push-along toys will help your baby to learn to walk. On the other hand, she may prefer to sit and explore her books and toys. Whatever she enjoys, encourage her and give her lots of praise." *Annabel*

new things I can do ....

....

my best sounds or first words ....

....

....

my favorite person to cuddle ....

....

my favorite new toys ....

....

places I've been to ....

....

number of teeth ....

a photo of me
at 11 months

weight ....
length ....

months

"It's a magical milestone when your baby starts walking, and many babies take their first steps around one year. Your baby may also say one or two words. He'll love pretend play with a toy telephone, making scribbles with chunky wax crayons, and playing with stacking toys." *Annabel*

new things I can do ....
....

my words ....
....

my favorite television programs ....
....

funny things I do ....
....
....

foods I like ....
....

people I love ....
....

a photo of me
at 12 months

weight ....
length ....

my first birthday

" The first birthday marks the end of an extraordinary year, not just for your baby, but for you too—you have come so far. Your baby won't mind how you celebrate, but use these pages to record the memories of the special day. " Annabel

how I celebrated ....
....
....

presents I received ....
....
....

who came to visit ....
....
....
....

food I ate ....
....

my cake ....
....

Annabel's dark and white chocolate cupcakes

Instead of making a large birthday cake, I prefer to bake a collection of cupcakes, which are easier for babies to eat and look stunning arranged on a tiered cake stand with a candle on the top. Decorate with grated chocolate or colorful sprinkles.

ingredients

1oz (30g) dark chocolate

¼ cup butter, at room temperature

⅓ cup dark brown sugar

1 large egg, beaten

½ tsp vanilla extract

4 tbsp sour cream

½ cup all-purpose flour

2 tbsp cocoa powder

1 heaping tsp baking powder

a good pinch of salt

¼ cup chocolate chips

white chocolate frosting

2oz (60g) white chocolate

¼ cup lightly salted butter, softened

½ cup confectioners' sugar, sifted

1 tsp pure vanilla extract

a little dark chocolate, grated, or ¼ cup of sprinkles, for decoration (optional)

1 Preheat the oven to 350°F. Line a small muffin pan with 8 paper cupcake cases.

2 Break up the dark chocolate, put it in a ovenproof bowl over a pan of simmering water, and stir until melted. Alternatively, microwave on high for 1½–2 minutes. Stir and allow to cool for 5 minutes.

3 Cream the butter and brown sugar in a bowl until fluffy, then beat in the cooled chocolate, followed by the egg, vanilla, and sour cream.

4 Sift the flour, cocoa, baking powder, and salt into the bowl and fold in. Finally fold in the chocolate chips.

5 Spoon into the paper cupcake cases (about two-thirds full). Bake for 18–20 minutes, until risen and the centers spring back when lightly touched. Cool thoroughly on a wire rack.

6 To make the frosting, melt the white chocolate in the same way as before and allow to cool. Beat the butter, sugar, and vanilla together until smooth then beat in the cooled chocolate. Swirl the frosting over the cold cakes and decorate with a little grated chocolate or some sprinkles.

makes 8 cupcakes

suitable for freezing—without frosting

preparation time: 20 minutes plus chilling time

cooking time: 18–20 minutes

about the author

Annabel Karmel is the leading author on cooking for children and has now written 15 best-selling books which are sold all over the world. She writes regularly for national newspapers and appears frequently on radio and television as the UK's top expert on children's nutritional issues. She now has her range of "make your own" equipment and food to help mothers prepare fresh baby food as well as "Eat Fussy" chilled ready meals. Annabel was awarded an MBE for services to child nutrition in 2006.

For further information on Annabel's titles and food ranges, please visit Annabel's own web-site www.annabelkarmel.com

Author acknowledgments

I'd like to thank Peggy Vance for believing in me and making this book happen, Helen Murray for all her hard work, and Sara Kimmins and Peggy Sadler for such a beautiful keepsake. Also my dear friend Caroline Stearns, who is always on hand for advice, and my children Nicholas, Lara and Scarlett for teaching me so much about the joys of motherhood, ... and making me cherish the memories. We still have fun looking back ....

Publisher's acknowledgments

The publisher would like to thank Carolyn Humphries for recipe testing, Constance Novis for Americanizing, and the following for their kind permission to reproduce their photographs: iStockphoto.com: Steven Davidi p.3 (foot); Ute Hil p.3 (hand).

All other images © Dorling Kindersley
For further information see: www.dkimages.com